GLASGOW SINCE 1900

ROYAL EXCHANGE

1. Royal Exchange by Henri Cassiers (1901).

BUCHANAN STREET

2. Buchanan Street by Henri Cassiers (1901).

GLASGOW
SINCE
1900

3. St Vincent Street: St Columba's Church reflected in the Britoil headquarters building.

Paul Harris

LOMOND BOOKS

First published by Archive Publications Ltd 1989
Reprinted 1994 by Lomond Books
36 West Shore Road
Granton
Edinburgh

Printed in the Republic of Slovenia by Gorenjski Tisk Printing Co., Kranj

© Copyright text and arrangement Paul Harris 1994

ISBN 948946 70 9

4. Sauchiehall Street by night.

CONTENTS

ACKNOWLEDGEMENTS

All the pictures in this book come from the files of The Scotsman Publications Ltd, with the exception of those noted below, and I am most grateful to Andrew Harton and to Brenda Woods and her staff in the library for their assistance.

Pictures numbered 13, 16, 18, 19, 20, 21, 22, 23, 24, 25, 26, 66, 67, 73, 83, 88, 91 and 165 all come from the Archive Publications Ltd collection. Those numbered 1, 2, 11, 12, 32, 33, 36, 37, 38, 39, 40, 41, 42, 43, 44, 80, 81, 92, 93, 122, 125, 149, 150, 196, 221 and 222 are from my own collection. I am grateful to Messrs T & R Annan & Sons of Glasgow for their cooperation and photographs 14, 15, 29, 151, 168, 178 and 223 are drawn from their archives. Other pictures have been kindly supplied by The Fine Art Society Ltd (front cover), Scottish Television (112), BBC Scotland (120), Tennent Caledonian Breweries (86, 87, 163) and Barclay Lennie (45, 46, 123).

For their assistance with my researches my thanks go particularly to Barclay Lennie, Lawrance Black, Bill Brady and Douglas Annan.

Paul Harris

October 1989

INTRODUCTION

It would be a very perverse observer indeed who failed to admit that Glasgow *is* different. Glasgow inspires affection, amuses and infuriates like no other city in Scotland. The mention of Glasgow in some far flung foreign city can be calculated to produce an emotional response, a burst of bonhomie and a flood of reminiscence which few other cities engender. Who on earth could become emotional about Edinburgh, for example? The late Colm Brogan wrote in 1952: "A couple of years ago I attended a penitential affair called a dinner dance, in a London hotel. The guests were firmly requested not to sing to the music of the band. They observed this instruction so faithfully that very few of them showed any inclination even to dance. All went merry as a passing bell, until the band struck up *I belong to Glasgow*. Almost on the instant the dance floor was crowded with vigorously whirling couples and everybody was singing, including the band". (*The Glasgow Story*).

The unaffected words of Will Fyffe (118) are written direct from the heart — some might say without reference to the head — but the message is enduring:

I belong to Glasgow,
Dear old Glasgow toun.
But what's the matter with Glasgow?
For it's going round and round.
I'm only a common old working chap,
As anyone here can see,
But when I get a couple of drinks on a
Saturday,
Glasgow belongs to me.

Of course, Glasgow is different. Can you imagine a roomful of people in London, New York or wherever rising to their feet and singing "I belong to Edinburgh"? Never in a thousand years.

To encapsulate the story of Glasgow this century in 250 photographs and a few thousand words is well nigh impossible. The problem is not so much what to put in but what to leave out. This book inevitably is a highly subjective collection of images which will, hopefully, give something of the flavour of the changes and the fluctuations in fortunes which have alternately beset and favoured the city. The decay of traditional industry to the rise of a new and vigorous service economy (or "bistro economy", as one commentator critically observed). The perceived poverty of areas like the now much romanticised Gorbals area, razed to the ground and resurrected disastrously in the tower block syndrome (198-207). The incredible artistic and cultural vitality of the city at the turn of the century as what was to become known internationally as 'The Glasgow Style' flowered and flourished alongside its maestro, Charles Rennie Mackintosh (27, 28, 30-44). For Glasgow, 1990, its recognition as City of Culture is actually coming a full ninety years late. It is not Glasgow which awakens but the rest of the world.

It is often said that the year 1901 ushered in a new era with the death of Queen Victoria. Yet the death of the Queen did not have quite the same effect on the Second City of the Empire as it did on London. There was a certain firmness of purpose, a deep-rooted sense of direction and such enormous confidence in Glasgow that she continued with her multi-faceted existence seemingly untouched: artists painted; architects designed; the wealthy commercial classes patronised the arts (at least, those they understood); the great 1901 Exhibition in Kelvingrove Park and environs attracted a staggering three million plus visitors (122-4); and the Clyde busied itself with turning out great liners like the ill-fated *Lusitania* (93), started in 1904 and completed within a staggering 14 months.

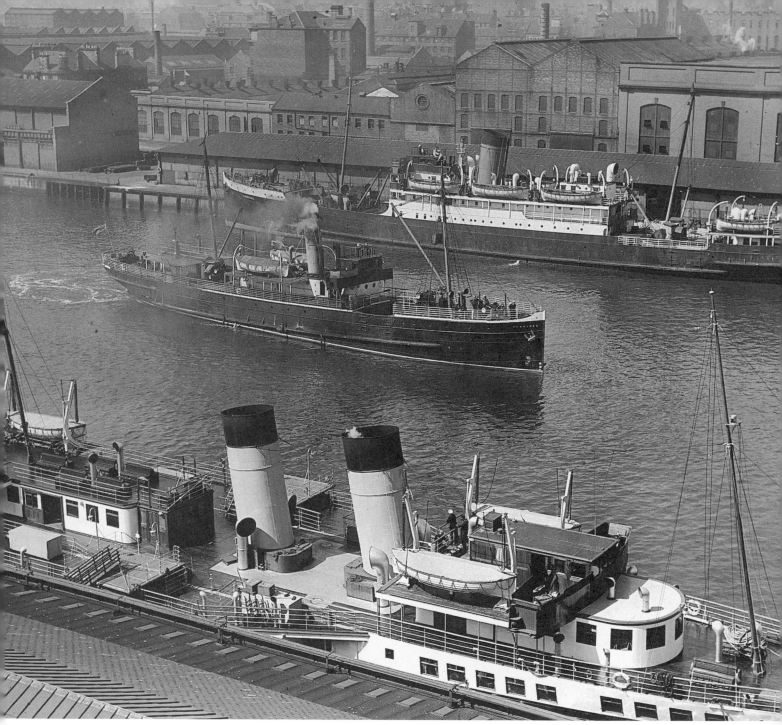

5. A bustling river scene on the Clyde near King George V Bridge in this 1957 photograph.

6. *above:* Argyle Street and the famous 'Hielanman's Umbrella' which carried the old Caledonian Railway out of Central Station (1959).

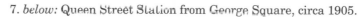

7. *below:* Queen Street Station from George Square, circa 1905.

Through the medium of the photograph we are able to observe the rapid changes in society this century much better than in any previous era. Changes in dress and fashion can be instantly assimilated: the differences between the barefoot children in Elder Park in 1900 and their counterparts in 1988 are clear for all to see (151, 152). The boaters at Central Station (178), the hooped skirts in Sauchiehall Street (16) and the barefoot children of the East End (17) allow us all to draw our own conclusions based upon the visual evidence provided. With the photograph, physical changes can be instantly discerned. Changes in dress, transport, shops and places of work are all dramatically revealed. Whilst I would never subscribe to the dictum that the camera never lies, for it frequently can be made to do so, I would yet maintain that it is singularly effective in capturing a moment in time for later consideration. As every Picture Editor on any newspaper knows, a good picture is worth a thousand words and my selection procedure in choosing the images for this book has been based upon the search for that type of image: the picture which does not simply and baldly portray some event but which tells us something more, whether in the gestures and expressions of those photographed or the actual composition by the photographer as *he* tries to tell us something about his subject.

Photographs of buildings long gone or recently built are fascinating enough in themselves but, for me, pale into insignificance against images like those of the scene outside the Locarno in 1965 (194), the packed stand at the Rangers ground at the turn of the century (159), the reading room at the Mitchell Library in 1911 (29) or the waiting room at the Royal Infirmary in Edwardian times (223). These photographs can actually tell us something — whether it be about the aimlessness of youth, the special occasion that was once a football match, the thirst for knowledge that characterised some eras or the rather unchanging nature of the health service. There have been many books featuring the architecture and buildings of what was an incomparable Victorian city. But there have been remarkably few 'people books' featuring the life and work of the Glaswegian during this century.

There have been some areas which I have deliberately excluded. Glasgow's experience during the Second World War is represented by only the two images: Alexander MacPherson's unusual pencil drawing of War Weapons Week in George Square in November 1940 (f.c.) and Ian Fleming's particularly graphic oil painting of the unearthing of victims of the Maryhill tenement collapse in Kilmun Street in March 1941 (221). For the seeker of images of Glasgow during that war there is *Glasgow at War* (Paul Harris/ Archive Publications 1986) and *Scotland at War* (Ian Nimmo/Archive Publications 1989). More recently, a number of skilful photographers have successfully tackled Glasgow through the medium of what I would term the 'art photograph': Oscar Mazaroli in *Shades of Grey*, Colin Baxter in *Aerial Pictures* and Joseph MacKenzie in *Gorbals Children*. Again, I have not concerned myself with their work. Far from demeaning such work of extraordinarily high quality, they are, again, readily available elsewhere and it is the object of this present book to pull together between two covers a range of pictures otherwise not readily available.

Most of the photographs here have appeared previously in newspapers like *The Scotsman*, *The Weekly Scotsman* and *Scotland on Sunday*. They are essentially ephemeral images. They appeared once in a newspaper, were possibly used the next day to wrap a portion of fish and chips and the images were effectively discarded — surviving only deep in a newspaper archive for possible re-use but, more likely, destined for oblivion. The object here is to revive these images and to give them the chance of some less ephemeral use. This is sometimes simply called nostalgia. But this is something of a pejorative term which devalues the concept. We are all, for better or for worse, fascinated by where we came from and by what happened in our present surroundings in recent times. I don't think there is any need to be defensive about this. Quite the contrary, I think such interest can be clearly construed as being indicative of a whole range of positive virtues from civic pride to family unity.

This book is of the "Gosh, I remember that!" variety. We find it generally satisfying and fulfilling to reminisce over things experienced directly or second-hand. So, to that activity this book is what the board and cards are to *Trivial Pursuits*. It is something to gather around and use as the basis for a well-worn, tried and tested game.

The medium of the photograph as a historical document came early to Glasgow. The photographers T & R Annan were established in 1855 — originally as Berwick & Annan, then a few years later Robert

Annan joined his brother Thomas in the firm after Berwick's departure. One of their most famous and accomplished ventures was the production in 1868, for the City of Glasgow Improvement Trust, of a series of albumen prints in bound presentation volumes depicting the squalor and poverty of the poorer parts of the city. Throughout the following decades Annans continued to portray the city, and a number of images in this book (14, 15, 29, 151, 168, 178 and 123) are drawn from their collection of 12 x 8 in. and 8 x 6 in. glass plates in the period 1900-1914 which preserve such high quality images of the life of the city.

The Aberdeen photographer, George Washington Wilson, started to work in the city during the 1860s and although he retired in 1888 his firm continued to photograph the streets and buildings until the early

8. Feeding the pigeons in George Square in the 1950s.

years of this century. The Washington Wilson output was, however, primarily touristic in intent and is not so concerned with any form of social comment.

The rise of the picture postcard brought photographic images into the hands of a much larger public. Many of the images of Glasgow in the early years of this century used here are taken from postcard views. The picture postcard was introduced in 1894 and from 1902 the Post Office permitted the use of the divided back card which allowed all of the front to be used for the picture (messages hitherto having been scribbled around or across the actual picture) and both message and name and address to be inscribed on the reverse side. Picture postcards poured onto the market. They were far more widely used than they are today and filled many more functions than those of

simply imparting greetings from the seaside. I have one view of Sauchiehall Street stamped 9.30 am during 1905 and bearing the confident message: "This is just to let you know that I simply cannot make it to tea today . . ."

A series of particularly attractive views of Glasgow during the 1901 Exhibition were painted by the Belgian landscape and marine artist Henri Cassiers who travelled to the city and whose work was reproduced on coloured postcards now much prized by collectors (1, 2, 11, 12, 80, 122). There were many publishers of postcards set up in the city and every imaginable subject was tackled as people began to collect as well as send cards.

Photographs were still not widely used in

9. April Showers, Gordon Street, in the early '50s.

10. Charing Cross, May 1958.

newspapers and the photograph was sometimes the only readily available means of obtaining a picture of a significant event. Just as in the 1980s, royal visits (23), weddings and birthdays (12) and ships (92, 93) were popular. Many businesses used the postcard as a form of cheap and effective advertising, like the agency promoting the young, bemedalled dancers (22). Photographs of some music hall stars were in such demand that, in desperation, some unscrupulous publishers superimposed photographs of the face of the popular Gertie Millar on images of other women's bodies. She sued but lost in the somewhat different climate of Edwardian times.

By the 1920s the postcard boom was over. The best quality postcards had often been printed in Germany, although published at home, and, of course,

the Kaiser's war had cut off supplies. Social conditions were changing rapidly and the Post Office misguidedly doubled the postage rate for cards, effectively killing the goose that had laid the golden egg. The development of roll film — as opposed to the use of the cumbersome glass plate — was soon to make snapshots and photography available to a much wider, although predominantly middle class, market. It is still curious, however, to note how few images seem to survive of many basic, everyday activities.

Most photographs which are taken are of family groups and then, most often, on holiday. Comparatively few photographers until very recently took photographs of their work and leisure activities with a view to recording for posterity. Good, candid social images are difficult to find and, again until very recently, old photographs tended to be disposed of by private and public owners alike. Great archives of photographic plates have been destroyed rather than the space given up to retain them. Much has ended up in skips and for other material the end has been just as ignominious. A Glasgow librarian told me several years ago of his efforts to track down a major collection of glass plates from the 1930s and '40s. Arriving at a smart house in the suburbs, he asked if he might see the plates. The owner proudly took him through the house to the back and pointed to his new greenhouse — every pane representing one scrupulously cleaned glass plate.

Many of the pictures in this book come under the broad category of "news photographs". These do tend to get retained by newspapers, although in the best kept offices there are some seemingly inexplicable omissions. Glasgow has been the setting for some of the most dramatic stories in British newspaper history and these are well represented: the Cheapside whisky bond blaze (238), the James Watt Street fire (241) and the Ibrox disaster (235).

Then there are dramatic events which because in substance they happen in private, behind closed doors, only photograph in a limited way. The operations of characters like Peter Manuel (226), Paddy Meehan (229), Jimmy Boyle (230) and Oscar Slater (224) are dramatic in themselves but, by their nature, are rarely photographed in the occurrence, like the dramatic razor slashing picture (239) which is rendered extraordinary by its very rarity as a species. We may get a glimmer from the mad, staring eyes of Peter Manuel or the disgruntled mien of Meehan, but here the photograph can only hint at the story.

Here, then, is some ninety years of Glasgow through the camera lens and the eyes of a few painters. This is essentially a *pot pourri*. Open it up and take out what you will. There is much that is not here: to work out what is missing may be as much fun for the reader as enjoying what is here!

DAWN OF A
NEW CENTURY

11. Trongate by Henri Cassiers (1901).

12a. Charing Cross, Glasgow, 1905.

12b. Mark Ardkinglas, Glasgow's oldest inhabitant at
105 years of age, pictured in 1905.

. A certain *joie de vivre* is evident in this popular Edwardian postcard which was posted 1905.

Horse-drawn cabs and electric trams dominate the traffic at Charing Cross, 1914.

15. St Vincent Place looking towards George Square, 1900. Architecturally, this scene has changed remarkably little in 90 years.

16. Union Street, circa 1900.

17. East end character 'Old Bob' and the children at the Glasgow Corporation Sanitary Department playground in Bain Square, Calton, circa 1914.

18. This scene, circa 1900, in the old High Street contrasts sharply with the affluence and opulence of the commercial areas of the city. The pawnbroker's sign features prominently in the foreground.

19. The street traffic at Glasgow Cross in 1900 reflects changing times.

20. Electric trams on the Jamaica Street Bridge, 1900.

21. Buchanan Street, circa 1910.

22. An extraordinary advertising card, issued in 1905, for the bemedalled dancing duo, Retta and Rex, 'The Dancing Marvels'.

23. Visit of the Prince and Princess of Wales to Glasgow, 23 April 1907.

POSTCARD VIEWS OF EDWARDIAN GLASGOW

24. Argyle Street looking east.

25. The University and Kelvingrove Park.

26. Kelvin Bridge and Great Western Road, looking east.

27. *above:* Glasgow School of Art: the enduring symbol of the genius of its architect, Charles Rennie Mackintosh. It was completed in 1899.

28. *right:* Scotland Street School, also by Charles Rennie Mackintosh, completed in 1906.

29. The Reading Room at the Mitchell Library, 1911. The desire for self-improvement was a feature of the time.

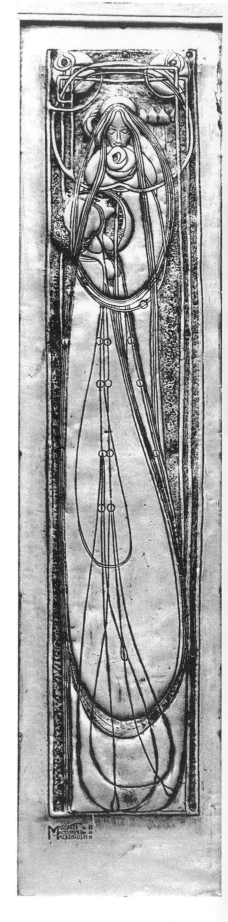

30. *above:* Within the Hunteran Art Gallery, Glasgow University recreated the house of Charles Rennie Mackintosh. The skilful reconstruction was completed in September 1981 and this photograph shows the drawing-room complete with many original furnishings and fittings.

31. *above right:* A silver lead panel (1901) by Margaret Macdonald Mackintosh entitled 'The Dew' which was originally installed in the Ingram Street tea-room.

THE·GLASGOW·LECTVRE·ASSOCIATION

A·RAEBVRN·

32. The Mackintoshes were the best known exponents of the distinctive design movement which was to become known as 'The Glasgow Style'. But there were also a large number of lesser known artists. This poster for the Glasgow Lecture Association was by Agres Raeburn, circa 1900, and used the Celtic motif of the snake.

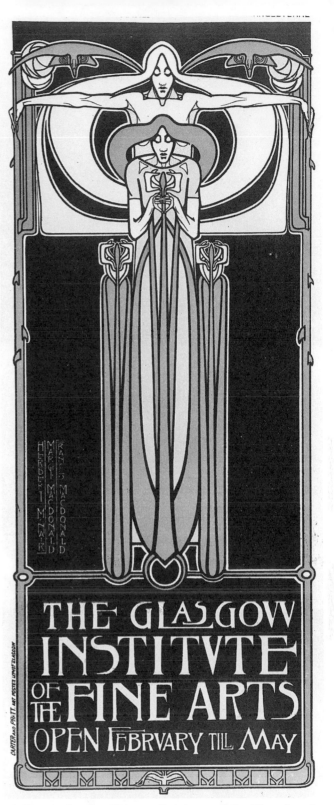

THE GLASGOW INSTITVTE OF THE FINE ARTS OPEN FEBRVARY TILL MAY

33. Poster for the Glasgow Institute of the Fine Arts by sisters Margaret and Frances Mackintosh and Herbert Macrair.

THERE'S A LOT GLASGOWING ON IN 1990.

EUROPEAN CITY OF CULTURE

34. The influence of the 'Glasgow Style' is very much apparent in this 1989 design for a motif for the 'European City of Culture', 1990.

36. *above:* Jessie M King's title page for *The City of the West* published by T N Foulis in 1911. This whimsical study of Glasgow was enormously successful and is now a collector's item in its original edition.

35. *left:* George Younger, Secretary for Scotland, inspects the Mackintosh Furniture Room at the Glasgow School of Art together with the Principal, Professor Anthony Jones, December 1982.

37. *above:* A Mackintosh token projects above the railings at the Glasgow School of Art.

38. *right:* A leaflet designed in 1907 by Jessie M King for Henry Wise's *Arcadian Restaurant*. The drawing is typical of J M King's work while the lettering is derived from Mackintosh.

39. A bedroom design by George Logan from the Wylie and Lochhead catalogue: the ultimate in style for the Glasgow connoisseur, circa 1905.

40. The Argyle Street tea-rooms were featured in *The Studio* of October 1906, as international recognition of the 'Glasgow Style' was achieved.

Modern Decorative Art at Glasgow

ORNER OF LUNCHEON ROOM AT MISS CRANSTON'S
EA HOUSE, ARGYLE STREET, GLASGOW

DECORATIONS BY GEORGE WALTON
FURNITURE BY C. R. MACKINTOSH

41. A watercolour by Meg Wright, dated 1901, depicting a Glasgow embroidress.

Margaret Gilmour, who had studios at West George [Str]eet, was an accomplished and prolific metal worker. [Thi]s charming photograph frame was typical of her work.

43 This design by Charles Rennie Mackintosh for a tester bed (1900) was remarkably similar to the European Secessionist designs of the time.

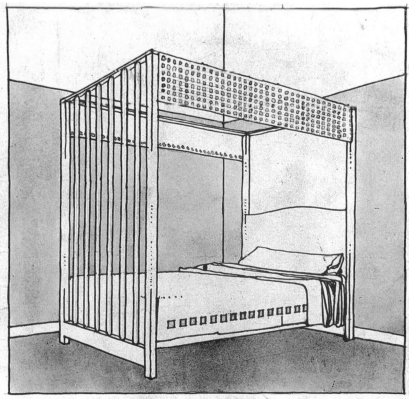

44. The doorway designed by Charles Rennie Mackintosh for the Lady Artists' Club in Blythswood Square (1908). It was a remarkable combination of his modern 'squared' forms and classical motifs, and thus fitted admirably within a Georgian Style terrace.

45. Cover of *Official Guide to Glasgow & Neighbourhood by the Tramway Car Routes.*

46. Copeland & Lye department store by Tom Gilfillan, circa 1950.

47. Looking down Union Street at the junction of Renfield Street and Gordon Street.

top, opposite page: Christmas decorations light the way for shoppers in Sauchiehall Street.

bottom, opposite page: This December 1958 scene in Argyle Street reminds us of the days before Clean Air Acts when fog was a regular feature Glaswegian life.

above left: 'The Barras', circa 1955.

above right: The John Lewis department store, Argyle Street in the 1950s, proudly sports the notice: "You can be x-rayed at Lewis's".

below: The striking modern post-war architecture of Boots' department store, Argyle Street, housed the famous meeting point known as 'Stand Corner', such has been the number of still-born romances it has witnessed!

53. Book store at the 'Barras'.

54. The old Fish Market in 1982 before its ill-fated conversion into the Briggait Shopping Centre.

55. *above:* The wholesale fruit and vegetable market at Candleriggs which ceased in April 1969.

56. *below:* A scene typical of Glasgow's famous 'Barras' market shortly after the turn of the century.

57. *below:* Little seems to have changed in this recent photograph of Paddy's Market, under the arches of the old Glasgow and South-Western railway.

58. *left:* The massive bulk of the St Enoch Shopping Centre, opened May 1989.

59. *bottom, opposite page:* The Victorian magnificence of the St Enoch Station and Hotel once occupied the site in St Enoch Square.

60. *below left:* Demolition of the St Enoch Hotel (1978).

61. *right:* More than one Glasgow wag has called the St Enoch Centre "Europe's Largest Greenhouse". Nevertheless, its design is very much in the mainstream of European and North American design for such shopping centres.

62. *below right:* Not all modern shopping centres are a success. The Briggait, located in the old fish market, was seen as Glasgow's answer to Covent Garden. It opened in February 1986 and closed just two years later.

63. Sauchiehall Street in the rain as the pedestrian precinct is opened, summer 1988.

64, 65. Views down Sauchiehall Street: the original Daly's store is shrouded in scaffolding as the developers move in. The new store is on the left.

66. Sauchiehall Street at the turn of the century, a new electric tram in the foreground. The street is now lit by electric arc lights. In the background, on the left, is Copeland & Lye's department store.

67. *right:* Renfield Street, Glasgow. R W Forsyth's department store can be seen on the corner.

68. *bottom right:* The stylish Beresford Hotel at 460 Sauchiehall Street was built to house visitors to the 1938 Exhibition. There were 198 bedrooms (one bathroom to every four bedrooms — a considerable luxury!) and rooftop dog kennels, but its moment of glory was short-lived for the outbreak of war meant the end for the establishment. It is now Strathclyde University's Baird Hall of Residence.

69. *above left:* Glasgow's last procession of tramcars leaves the Dalmarnock Depot headed by an old horse tram (1955).

70. *right:* The last of Glasgow's trolleybuses sets off from George Square on its final run (May 1967).

71. *below left:* In 1980 the closure of the Kelvinhaugh Ferry was announced, bringing to an end the 800 year-old ferry service across the river at Queen's Dock. At the time of the closure decision, only 67 people per day were using the historic service.

72. *above right:* The first electric train leaves Queen Street Station for Helensburgh (1960).

73. *below right:* The Botanic Gardens Station, circa 1910. It was burnt down in 1970.

74. *above left:* This 1978 photograph shows modernisation work on the Glasgow underground: the first escalator is installed at Kelvinbridge Station.

75. *above right:* An original (1896) underground car brought out of retirement and seen here at Hillhead Station.

76. *left:* Inside one of the underground cars which were introduced in 1980.

77. *below right:* The modernised Buchanan Street Station is opened to the public, March 1980.

78. In April 1966 a new phenomenon was introduced to the Glasgow motorist —
the yellow-painted box junction. The first one, seen here, was at the junction o
Hope Street and St Vincent Street.

79. Construction work on the Clyde Tunnel.

AT WORK

SHIPYARDS ON THE CLYDE

80. Shipyards on the Clyde by Henri Cassiers (1901).

81. Battlefield Road, Glasgow, 1925.

82. Newly built locomotives, fresh from the works of the North British Locomotive Company, are hauled through the streets of Glasgow bound for the docks.

83. Springburn Fire Brigade parade in front of a tank built at the Cowlairs Works for a flag day in aid of the war effort, May 1917.

84. Women's First World War work: the Corporation of Glasgow Gas Department. Sixteen women were employed during the war in cleaning fire bricks.

85. Women's First World War work: the Corporation of Glasgow Tramways Department. Seven women were employed as switch pillar inspectors.

86. The J & R Tennent Pavilion at the 1938 Empire Exhibition in Bellahouston Park. Draught Tennents Lager was sold here for the very first time.

87. In 1985 Tennents celebrated their centenary at Wellpark Brewery, Glasgow. Here Tennents Lager 'Lovely' Janis Sue Smith is pictured with an 1885 stoneware lager flask, a 1985 can and a 1935 'Brasso' style can.

Largest Crane in the World-height 170 feet, length of jib 258 feet, lifting capacity 250 tons - Fairfield Shipbuilding Yard, Govan.

88. The Fairfield shipbuilding yard at Govan, dominated by what was for long the largest crane in the world: 170 feet high with a jib length of 258 feet and lifting capacity of 250 tons.

89. Lithgows yard, 1970.

90. A view from times past: plenty of work on the stocks at Fairfields yard.

91. Breaking for the dinner hour at John Brown's Clydebank yard, circa 1920.

Dinner Hour, John Brown's Yard, Clydebank

92. The Clyde Steamship Company was but one of Glasgow's operators in the busy transatlantic passenger trade before the First World War.

CLYDE STEAMSHIP CO.

S. S. HURON

General Offices: Pier 36 North River · Branch 290 Broadway · New York

93. The ill-fated *Lusitania* was a Clyde-built ship launched in June 1906.

Cunard Liner, "Lusitania," (Turbine).

Torpedoed and sunk by German Submarine off the Old Head of Kinsale, on the South Coast of Ireland, on 7th May, 1915.

32,000 Tons ; 68,000 H.P. ; Speed, 26½ knots. Length, 787 ft. ; Breadth, 88 ft. ; Depth, 60 ft.

94. *above:* The 1971 work-in at Upper Clyde Shipbuilders has joined the legends of British trade unionism alongside the Tolpuddle Martyrs and Red Clydeside of the 1920s. Here, work-in leader and shop steward Jimmy Reid addresses the assembled workforce after the government decides to force UCS into liquidation.
95. *below left:* A dramatic banner for the work-in.
96. *below right:* The launch of anti-submarine frigate HMS *Yarmouth* at John Brown's yard in 1959.
97. *top, opposite page:* One of the Clyde's proudest moments, the launch of the liner *Queen Mary* in September 1934.
98. *bottom left, opposite page:* The *Queen Mary* sails down the Clyde, 25 March 1936.
99. *bottom right, opposite page:* The Cunard freighter *Carinthia* takes shape, 1955.

100. *top, opposite page:* The Union Castle liner *Transvaal Castle* nears completion at John Brown's Clydebank yard, December 1960.

101. *middle, opposite page:* Launch of the *Empress of Britain*, June 1955.

102. *below, opposite page:* The destroyer HMS *Hampshire* in the Clyde, March 1961, after her launch by Princess Margaret.

103. *above:* The *Queen Elizabeth II*, last of the great Cunarders, undergoes completion, December 1965.

104. The Queen Mother acknowledges the cheers of the crowd at the launching of the *British Queen* at John Brown's, September 1959.

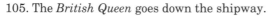
105. The *British Queen* goes down the shipway.

106. Launch of the Royal Yacht *Britannia* from John Brown's in 1953.

107. More than 300 people are involved in a community theatre project for Glasgow 1990 under the direction of playwright Tom McGrath and TAG Theatre.

108. *top left, opposite page:* Bill Paterson in the Glasgow-based ice-cream war feature film *Comfort and Joy*.

109. *top right, opposite page:* The popular singer Kenneth McKellar has always been strongly identified with Glasgow — not least as a result of his stirring rendering of *Song of the Clyde*.

110. *bottom, opposite page:* On location: author William MacIlvanney, creator of Glasgow fictional characters Laidlaw and Docherty. His novel *The Big Man* was contracted for a major feature film in 1989.

111. *right:* Scottish Television studios at the Theatre Royal, Cowcaddens, 1957.

112. *below:* An STV film crew on location in Glasgow with actor Mark MacManus, alias Taggart.

113. One of Scotland's first radio broadcasters, Kathle[en] Garscadden, known as Auntie Cyclone and Auntie Kathle[en] to generations of young Scots listeners to *Children's Hou[r]*. Here she is pictured with actress Mary Riggans at Rad[io] Clyde's recording of a programme about the early days [of] broadcasting.

114. In many respects, author and broadcaster Cliff Han[ley] is the personification of the Glaswegian with his paw[ky] humour and ready repartee. Here he dances in the stree[t] . . . again.

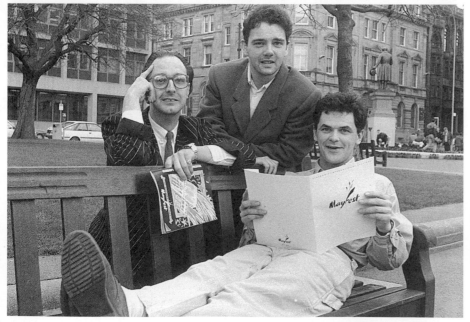

115. One of the more successful television comedy series [of] the 1980s was the Glasgow sitcom *City Lights* featuri[ng] Gerard Kelly, Simon Fanshawe and Pat Kane, who we[re] photographed in George Square in March 1988 to prom[ote] the expansion of Glasgow's Mayfest.

116. The artist and novelist Alasdair Gray, much acclaimed for his tangential view of the world — exemplified in his massive novel *Lanark* — photographed here by Jim Cunningham.

117. One of the most outstanding writers to emerge in Glasgow for several decades must be James Kelman, shortlisted for the prestigious Booker Prize in 1989.

118. Will Fyffe, Scots comedian and author of the world famous lyrics to the song *I Belong to Glasgow*.

119. Glasgow writer Lavinia Derwent, perhaps best known as the creator of 'Tammy Troot', opens an exhibition of paintings by children in Glasgow hospitals at Hillhead Library.

120. Jack House is one of the best known writers on Glasgow and his book *Square Mile of Murder*, about famous murder cases in the fashionable west end of the city, is regarded as a classic. In 1980, it was dramatised for television and here is pictured together with *left to right:* scriptwriter Joan Lingard, and actresses Gerda Stevenson, Morag Hood and Gwyneth Guthrie.

121. Key worker, rodent operative Smudge, the much loved cat at the People's Palace, pictured in the refurbished Winter Gardens.

EXHIBITION CITY

EXHIBITION ENTRANCE

122. Entrance to the 1901 Exhibition by Henri Cassiers (1901).

123a. 1901 Exhibition, *Kelvingrove, Glasgow,* by Robert McGown Coventry.

123b. *Old Scottish Street,* 1911 Exhibition, Kelvingrove.

124. The first of Glasgow's great exhibitions in this century was in 1901. The largest yet held in Britain, it covered 73 acres of Kelvingrove Park and the surrounding area. Here is James Miller's great baroque style Industrial Hall.

125. Kelvingrove Art Galleries were opened on the same day as the 1901 Exhibition. Until the galleries were bomb-damaged in 1941, the central feature was the sculpture court (seen here), now occupied with the dispensing of tea, coffee and souvenirs.

126. *above:* Construction work for the 1938 Empire Exhibition in Bellahouston Park. Here the Scottish Pavilion is under construction.

128. *top, opposite page:* The Palace of Engineering and the bandstand.

127. *below:* Workmen completing the Grand Staircase for the Exhibition.

129. *below:* The Empire Exhibition cost £10 million to mount in 1938 and the claim was made that "in conception, comprehensiveness and beauty it outrivals the most famous enterprises of the kind ever promoted". Alas, it was already overshadowed by the gathering war clouds in Europe.

130. *above:* All the fun of the fair on these ultra-modern roundabouts at the 19 exhibition.

131. *left:* Thomas Tait's dramatic tower built for the exhibition. It was demolish the following year lest it serve as a navigational aid for German bombers seeki Clydeside targets.

132. *top, opposite page:* Scottish Motor Show at the Kelvin Hall, circa 1964.

133. *bottom left, opposite page:* Exterior of the Kelvin Hall which was built on the s of the Machinery Hall of the 1901 Exhibition.

134. *bottom right, opposite page:* High-tech exhibition at the Kelvin Hall — 195 style.

137. The Festival site looking east from the tower.

138. Schoolchildren of Crookfur Primary cool off at the waterfall at the Glasgow Garden Festival.

135. This 180 degree photograph of the Glasgow Garden Festival site, 1988, taken from the top of the Clydesdale Bank Tower gives some idea of the size of the event. In the centre is the water basin and marina, and the River Clyde lies on the extreme left.

136. The Garden Festival was an enormous popular success in the tradition of all the great Glasgow exhibitions.

139, 140. The 1988 Garden Festival successfully combined images of Glasgow old and new and was, in itself, a symbol of regeneration in the ci

141. *left:* In December 1987 the main section the first footbridge across the Clyde for 1: years was lowered into place. The Bell's Bridg sponsored by the whisky firm, linked th Scottish Exhibition Centre site to the Garde Festival area.

142. *opposite page:* The ubiquitous Tennen lager girls at the Glasgow Garden Festival g the once over from tram driver Stanley Ker

143. In 1979 work was finally started on a building in Pollock Park to house the Burrell Collection of some 8,000 items given to the city in 1944. Dr Richard Marks, appointed the first keeper of the collection, is pictured on the building site.

144. The completed building for the Burrell Collection by architect Barry Gasson, 1983.

145. Her Majesty the Queen meets Sir William Burrell's daughter, Sylvia Burrell, at the opening of the Burrell Collection, October 1983.

146. Mayfest 1989 and Glasgow schools' youth chorus rehearses for the rock jazz opera *A Small Green Space*.

147. *above:* Scottish Exhibition Centre Open Day, August 1985.

148. *left:* Scottish Exhibition Centre complex from the air.

AT PLAY

149. *The Scotia Bar*, Stockwell Street, by Ernest Hood (1974).

150. *In a Pub, Glasgow* by Donald MacKenzie (1975).

151. *above:* Local children, Elder Park, Govan, circa 1900.

152. *left:* Local girls Allison Robertson, Laura Raskolnikoff and Caroline Haxton, Elder Park, Govan, publicising the 1986 Mayfest.

153. *left:* Buildings of the University of Glasgow reflected in the Kelvin.

154. *below left:* Student Vivienne Ennemoser was the first woman ever to get a drink in the previously all male preserve of Glasgow University Union in October 1980.

155. *below right:* This 1971 photograph shows the result of a ritual now sadly fallen out of fashion: the election of a Charities Queen. The winner here was 17 year old Angela Black, a student at Langside College of Further Education.

156. *top, opposite page:* Glasgow self-made businessman Sir Norman MacFarlane pictured with the Glasgow University debating team, 1988. *left to right:* Kevin Sneader, Austin Lally, Andrew McKie, David Rennie, Graeme Cleugh, Andrew Peterson and Kenneth Ritchie.

157. *bottom, opposite page:* Rag week 1973 and a flour bomb raid by University students on the Art College resulted in nine arrests on charges ranging from breach of the peace to police assault.

158. *opposite page:* The aftermath of the Rangers vs Celtic game at Hampden, May 1980.

159. *above:* The main stand at the Rangers ground, 1901.

160. *right:* Cup Final 1981 and Rangers carry off the cup.

161. *top, opposite page:* Celtic win the European Cup, May 1967.

162. *bottom, opposite page:* Celtic: cup-winners for the season 1988-89.

163. *above:* Promotion girls at the launch of the Tennent's Sixes, sponsored annually by Tennent Caledonian Breweries.

164. *below:* Partick Thistle captain Alex Rae with the League Cup after the historic 1971 victory over Celtic.

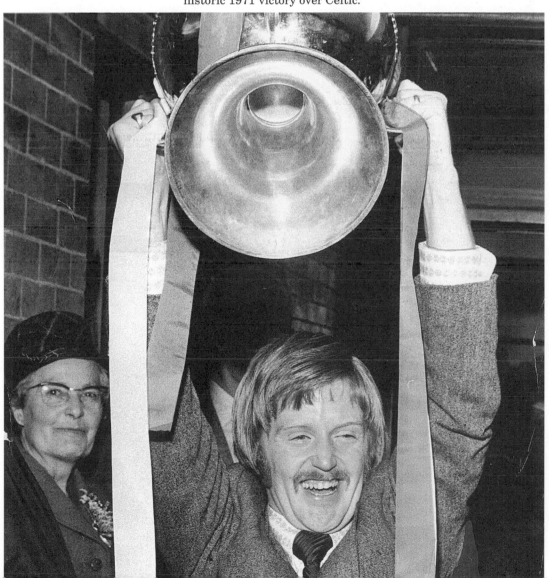

The River Clyde at Broomielaw, Glasgow

165. *top, left:* Doon the watter: the River Clyde at the Broomielaw, circa 1910.

166. *middle, left:* The Clyde steamer *St Columba* carries Glasgow Fair holidaymakers down the Clyde to Rothesay, 1959.

167. *bottom, left:* The ferry-steamer *Arran* leaves Dunoon for Gourock.

168. *main picture, right:* The paddle steamer *Eagle III* leaves Glasgow for "doon the watter", 1929.

169. *right:* Glasgow Fair 1960 and the *Maid of Argyll* leaves Rothesay.

170. *far right:* The Clyde pleasure steamer *Queen Mary II* leaves Glasgow, May 1960.

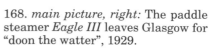

171. The last sea-going paddle steamer in the world — the PS *Waverley* — lies at her berth at Anderston Quay, 1987.

172. Miss Terry Corkill was the two millionth passenger to be carried aboard the refurbished PS *Waverley* since it was donated to the Paddle Steamer Preservation Society in 1974.

173. The PS *Waverley* in the Clyde, April 1959.

174, 175. Glasgow Fair holidaymakers arrive at Rothesay by steamer, 1959.

176. Renfrew Airport, 1955. A bold design for the time.

177. On the tarmac at Renfrew before the days of package holiday

178. Glasgow Fair Saturday at Central Station shortly after the turn of the century.

79. Exterior view of the Alhambra Theatre taken in the late '60s.

180. After the disastrous fire at the Alhambra in May 1971. The view from the side of the stage.

181. The famous 'Five past Eight' stage at the Alhambra. When it was first installed it was a modern marvel of its time with the revolving stages and bandstand which rose from the floor.

182. *top left:* Abandoned: Jimmy Logan's Metropole.

183. *top right:* Burnt out, 1961: Jimmy Logan's Metropole.

184. *middle left:* The magnificent interior of the Gorbals Palace before demolition began in 1977. Built in the 1880s as a music hall, it was converted into a theatre in 1907. After many years' use as a bingo hall, the roof fell in and a demolition order was placed on the building.

185. *middle right:* The Close Theatre, next door to the Citizens, was destroyed by fire in May 1973.

186, 187. *bottom left and right:* The Britannia Music Hall in Trongate started in 1865 as Trongate House and became the most popular music hall in the city during the Victorian and Edwardian periods.

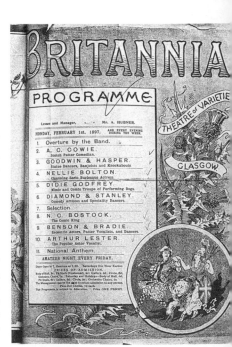

188. *top left:* The abandoned Appollo Theatre in Renfield Street, August 1986.

189. *middle left:* In 1988 a mysterious fire destroyed the top-storey former nightclub in the derelict Appollo Theatre, necessitating the demolition of the building. Another chapter in Glasgow theatre history had come to an end.

190. *bottom left:* The Empire Theatre.

191. *top right:* The Citizens Theatre.

192. *middle right:* Fire destroys the well-known Glasgow dance hall, The Albert, in the city's Bath Street.

193. *bottom right:* The Pavilion Theatre.

194. Saturday night dancing. Outside the Locarno, 1965.

195. October 1988 and a new type of nightspot comes to the city. A former British Rail Stranraer-Larne car ferry, the *Tuxedo Princess*, was brought from Newcastle and moored at Anderston Quay. Here Lord Provost Mrs Susan Baird pushes out the boat for the new "floating entertainment palace".

REGENERATION

196. Building in James Watt Street, rear view of redevelopment, 1989.

197. Redevelopment in the Merchant City: *above* before and *below* after.

198. The face of a bygone Glasgow. This picture shows Craigmaddie Lane off Sauchiehall Street in 1974.

199. Glasgow's Gorbals area before redevelopment.

200. Another scene now long gone: the gas lighter on the common stair in Glasgow's Gorbals.

201. Crown Street in the Gorbals, 1972, and new flats rise behind the old traditional tenement property.

202. Sandyfaulds Street in the Gorbals, 1960.

203. The end of the old familiar scene at Gorbals Cross, December 1975.

204. *above:* The high rise blocks which replaced more traditional housing in the 1960s and 1970s were often neither popular nor practical. This view shows the Red Road Flats after a fire high up in the block.

205. *above right:* Some flats were so unsuccessful that people refused to live in them. In 1987 the Hutcheson E Flats in the Gorbals were demolished only 12 years after being opened by The Queen. Despite the £8 million building cost, the construction was poor and the 12 blocks containing 756 houses became so damp the occupants were rehoused.

206. *below left:* This 1958 photograph of a new playground in the Gorbals was symbolic of the hope for a bright new future which was widespread at the time.
207. *below right:* Stark contrasts at Gorbals Cross, 1976.

208. *above:* Inner city regeneration at Ingram Square, 1986. Modern day Lord Provost Robert Gray with actors playing the part of Lord and Lady Provost Archibald (1762-4) in whose period of office the Square was originally built.

209. *top right:* The old Sherriff Court House in Ingram Street and now in the heart of the developing Merchant City. Currently the subject of ambitious plans for an international fashion centre with offices, retail and restaurant developments.

210. *middle:* Before: Custom House Quay as it used to be before becoming the subject of an environmental improvement scheme.

211. *right:* After: the Clyde Walkway.

212. Scheduled for redevelopment: Bell Street warehouse.

213. Scheduled for redevelopment: the former SCWS headquarters in Morrison Street, the subject of plans in 1989 to create a leisure, shopping and hotel development.

214. The old Wylie & Lochhead cabinet works in Kent Road, converted into flats.

215. A typical 1989 scene in the Merchant City quarter as old buildings are renovated and converted into flats.

216. Rebuilding the old St Andrews Halls, Granville Street, in 1975, which had been destroyed by fire.

217. This 1969 aerial photograph graphically illustrates the effect on the city of the urban motorway system and the building of the Kingston Bridge.

218. In the 1980s the creation of a seeming succession of new images for Glasgow has become a major industry all of its own. Rikki Fulton shows off the new East End promotion.

219. Dr Michael Kelly, former Lord Provost, and the phenomenally successful *Glasgow's Miles Better* logos.

220. The changing face of Glasgow in Allan Milligan's outstanding photograph of St Vincent Street (1988).

DIAL 999

221. *Rescue Party*, Kilmun Street, Maryhill, by Ian Fleming (1941).

222. St. Vincent Street, Glasgow,
1974 from an oil painting by Ernest Hood.

223. The waiting room at the Royal Infirmary, Glasgow, 1911.

224. Oscar Slater served 19 years of a life sentence for the murder of 83 year old Marion Gilchrist *(left)* at her Queen's Terrace flat. After years of sustained protest against his conviction — by eminent authorities of the like of Marshall Hall and Conan Doyle — he was vindicated and released.

225. Sir Percy Sillitoe is credited with breaking the power of the notorious Glasgow gangs. He was Chief Constable 1931-43 and went on to head MI5.

226. The face of a psychopath: Peter Manual. In May 1958 he was found guilty at the High Court in Glasgow of a string of murders involving young girls and the members of two families. This particularly evil and pathological murderer was executed two months later.

227, 228. The so-called Bible John murders remain unsolved to this day. A smartly dressed, Bible-quoting maniac who patronised the Barrowland Ballroom at Glasgow Cross did away with at least three women in the 1960s.

229. Glasgow underworld figure Paddy Meehan was convicted of murder but received a Royal Pardon after serving seven years of a life sentence. In 1989 he wrote and published his autobiography which was found to be so defamatory that bookshops declined to sell it and he was forced to take to the streets in order to find buyers. Here he is pictured at Central Station.

230. *left:* In November 1982 "baby-faced killer" Jimmy Boyle was released from prison after serving 15 years of a life sentence for murder. His stay inside has been frequently controversial: his work as an artist and sculptor in Barlinnie's Special Unit had excited much comment and during the currency of his sentence he had married social worker Dr Sarah Trevelyan, daughter of the former head of the British Board of Film Censors.

231, 232, 233. One of the most bizarre — and at times amusing — criminal cases ever heard in Glasgow concerned the Glasgow company Rotary Tools and its managing director J Maurice Cochrane who went down for 12 months. The sex and bribes trial heard daily of "bungs and benders" applied to grease the wheels of business as girls and money were supplied to customers. There was laughter in court when Miss Anna Grunt *(below right)* was called to give evidence of her activities. Cochrane was also accused of rigging a beauty competition so that Carolyn Schultz *(below left)* then his secretary and later his wife, might win it.

234. Police charge rioting fans at the May 1980 Rangers vs Celtic game at Hampden.

235. The Ibrox disaster. Sixty-six fans died on Stairway 13 on 2 January 1971 in the closing minutes of the traditional New Year derby match between Rangers and Celtic. Two goals in the final 60 seconds of the game caused pandemonium and excited fans tried to turn back with disastrous results.

238. The Cheapside whisky bond fire of March 1960 in which 19 firemen died after the walls of the building suddenly blew out.

236. *opposite page, top:* The St Andrews Halls are gutted by fire, November 1962.

237. *opposite page, left:* Firemen use a Clyde tug to fight a fire on a derelict pier at King George V Dock.

239, 240. This 1971 picture captured the moment as plainclothes Detective Inspector George Johnston was slashed by a youth with an open razor in Glasgow's Renfield Street. *inset:* The youth is subdued by uniformed officers. These pictures were published all over the world, contributing little to the improvement of the city's image abroad.

241. Twenty-two workers died behind the barred windows of the upholstery warehouse where they worked in
James Watt Street, November 1968.

242. The gutted shell of the 100-bedroom Grosvenor Hotel after the January 1978 blaze during the firemen's strike. Its owners, the Reo Stakis organisation, rebuilt the hotel remarkably successfully in its original style.

243. Smoke pours from the historic Ca'doro building at the corner of Gordon and Union Streets in March 1987.

244. The six-hour blaze at the Ca'doro building completely gutted it but reconstruction proved possible.

246. *above:* In November 1972 there was Glasgow's biggest tenement fire since the war when this block in Maryhill Road went up. More than 150 people were made homeless.

247. *right:* Army firemen — during the 1978 firemen's strike — tackle a blaze out of control in a building in South Portland Street, Gorbals, once used as a synagogue and more recently as the Irish Centre.

245. *left:* Fire at the Grandfare supermarket, Cowcaddens Street, in 1966.

248. Seven firemen were killed when the roof fell in on them as they fought this warehouse fire in Kilbirnie Street in August 1972.

249. Glasgow by Night (1): Renfield Street looking towards Union Street, 1983.

250. Glasgow by Night (2): River Clyde and city centre with RNVR sailing vessel *Carrick* in the foreground, 1988.

251. Glasgow by Night (3): Christmas decorations in George Square, 1959.